46698195R00061

Made in the USA
Middletown, DE
31 May 2019